ShortCuts

FOR FALL

Teacher Timesaver Charts, Patterns, Awards,
Newsletter, Calendars, Name Tags, Worksheets, and More

by Marilynn G. Barr

Monday Morning is a registered trademark of
Monday Morning Books, Inc.

Entire contents copyright © 1992
by Monday Morning Books, Inc., Box 1680,
Palo Alto, California 94302

For a complete catalog write to the address above.

ISBN 1-878279-43-2

Printed in the United States of America

Contents

Introduction

Rewarding your students' achievements, scheduling parent-teacher conferences, and preparing for open house are easy with the seasonal patterns, charts, open worksheets, worksheet display banners, substitute teacher agenda, name tags, file folder covers, awards, and diplomas in **ShortCuts for Fall**.

Welcome your students to class at the beginning of the year with the September Open House Door Display, Bulletin Board Displays, and Bulletin Board Characters and Borders on pages 5, 8-9, 14-19, and 20. Accompanying Birthday, Seating, and Attendance Charts make it easy to get off to a fresh start!

Bulletin Board Characters are designed to use with the name tags/flashcards for a hands-on skills practice bulletin board or to display spelling words, math facts, color words, numerals, etc. Duplicate enough characters for each student in your class. Have each child color and cut out his or her character and attach a straw or paint stirrer to the back for a hand puppet.

The Bulletin Board Borders are easy to cut out and can be used to frame bulletin board displays. They can also be made into student headbands for class plays, parties, or just for fun. To make headbands, supply each child with three strips of the same border. Have students color and cut out the strips and tape or staple together the ends to form a band to fit each child's head. For a new twist, have your class color enough strips to decorate the window frames in your classroom to match the bulletin board border.

The variety of notes on pages 23-27 can be used to correspond with parents.

Provide your students with weekly Calendar Friezes (pages 31-33) to take home for parents to keep track of happenings in school. Or, provide calendars for each child to keep track of weekly weather changes.

List children's birth dates on the two-piece Birthday Charts on pages 34-38. As an alternative, eliminate the messages and use these charts to list classroom helpers, super achievers, and citizenship recognition or to announce a special event or guest.

Scrapbook Pages are a favorite with children and parents. Have your students periodically color or cut out pictures of favorite things, memorable events, parties, and special interests to paste on the Scrapbook Pages. Or have each student use the pages to make a keepsake record of skills practice, achievements, and awards to bind between construction paper covers and decorate.

Double the use of each Seating Chart as a trail gameboard. Before reproducing, write Start at one corner, End at the opposite corner, and program a few spaces with rewards and/or consequences. Color the repeating pattern and supply pawns and a spinner or skills practice game cards. Children then play the game similar to the way they play Candyland.

You can also double the use of the Attendance Charts by creating crossword puzzles or maze games for your students. Eliminate each heading and paste a Bulletin Board Border strip over the listing column to dress up the crossword or maze.

Program the Open Worksheets on pages 51-56 for skills practice. Eliminate the lines on the Open Manuscript Worksheets and use as bulletin board displays, picture frames, or art project frames. For a rainy day filler activity, provide each child with his or her own Open Shape Worksheet, paste, and colored tissue paper. Have students tear the tissue paper into small pieces and paste them inside the shape. Overlapping the tissue creates a stained-glass effect and makes an attractive display for windows, bulletin boards, and seasonal take-home gifts.

Worksheet Display Banners make "good work" displays extra special. You can also eliminate the messages and use the banners to display seasonal posters, student of the week photographs, or classroom rules.

Newsletters that let parents know all about what their child is doing are easy to produce with Newsletter Covers and Section Titles on pages 60-61. The artwork is also a great companion to the Scrapbook Pages for a classroom annual filled with memories.

In addition to identifying types of work, File Folder Covers can also be used as mini seasonal coloring posters. To do this, eliminate the words and provide students with crayons and/or markers to color and decorate their posters.

Off to a Fresh Start!
WELCOME TO MY CLASS!

_____
Teacher

Welcome to the Pumpkin Patch

Teacher

Open House Door Display

Happy Thanksgiving and Welcome to

_____'s

Teacher

Class

Bulletin Board Displays

September

Bulletin Board Displays
October

Bulletin Board Displays
October

Bulletin Board Displays
November

Bulletin Board Displays
November

Bulletin Board Character
Beaver

Bulletin Board Character

Chipmunk

Bulletin Board Character

Fox

Bulletin Board Character
Raccoon

Bulletin Board Character
Squirrel

Bulletin Board Character

Turtle

Bulletin Board Borders
September

Bulletin Board Borders
October

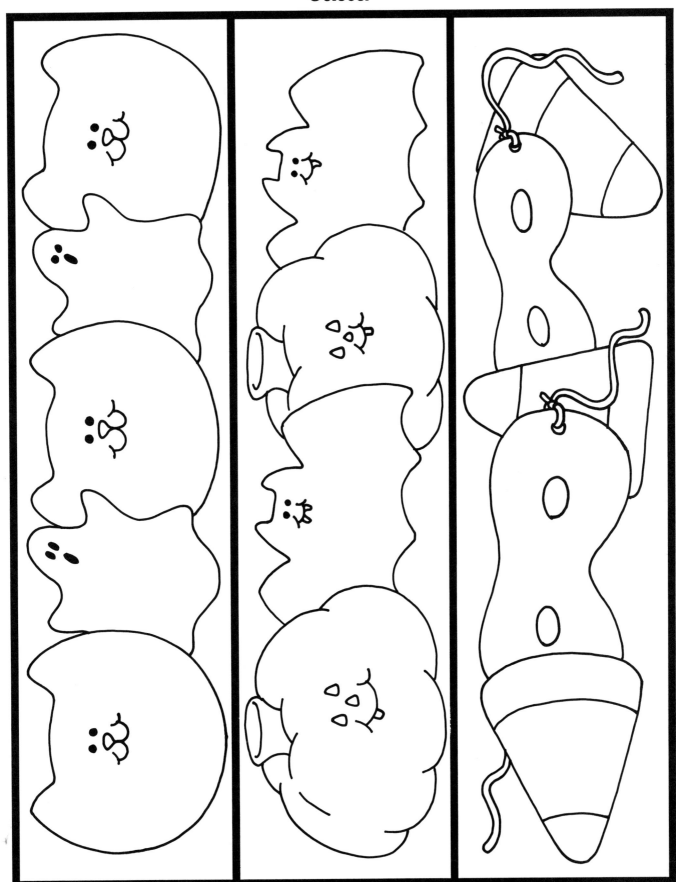

Bulletin Board Borders

November

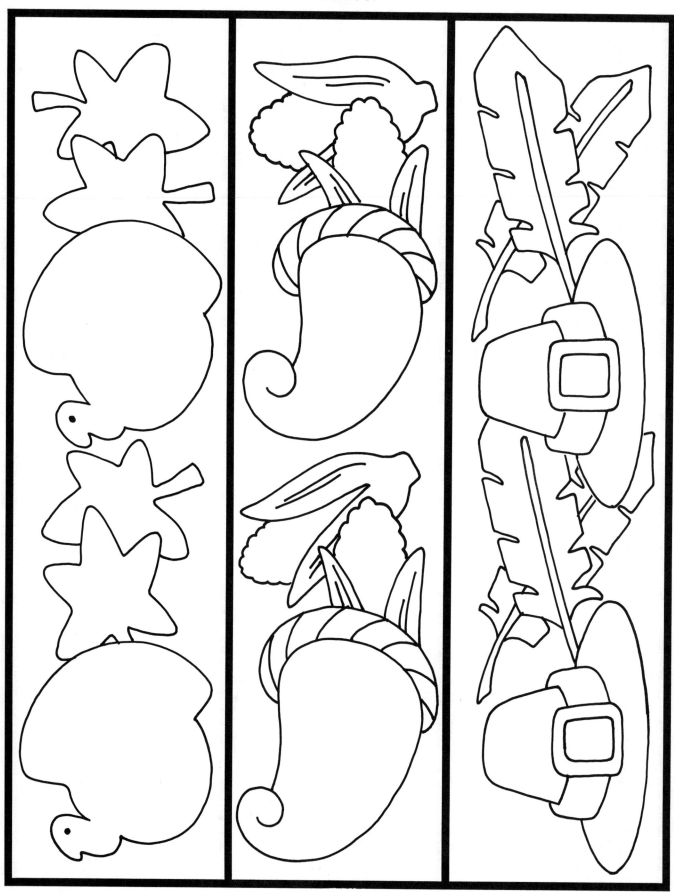

ShortCuts for Fall ©1992 Monday Morning Books, Inc.

Take-Home Progress Notes

_____
Student

is doing great work in

_____ .
Subject

_____
Date   Teacher

Please contact me to schedule a conference about ____'s progress.

_____
Student

_____
Teacher

_____
Telephone No.

_____
Date

_____
Student

has shown improvement in

_____ .
Subject

_____
Teacher

_____
Date

Improved!

_____
Student

needs to improve skills in

_____ .
Subject

_____
Date   Teacher

Thank You Notes

Your help is appreciated!

_____
Date

_____
Teacher

VOLUNTEERS ARE GREAT!
Thank you for sharing your time with us!

_____
Teacher

Thank You For All Your Hard Work!

_____
Date

_____
Teacher

Thank you! Thank you!

We couldn't have made it without you!

_____
Date

_____
Teacher

Homework Reminders

Homework
Reminder

Due Date

Homework
Reminder

Due Date

Homework
Reminder

Due Date

Open Notes to Parents

We are proud of

_____
Student

_____
Date

_____
Teacher

CONGRATULATIONS!

_____ has shown

_____
Student

_____
Date

_____
Teacher

_____ has shown

_____
Student

_____
Date

_____
Teacher

_____ is

_____
Student

_____
Date

_____
Teacher

Open Letter to Parents

Dear Parents,

Planning Calendar

September

September	Sunday	Monday	Tuesday	Wednesday	Thursday	Friday	Saturday

Planning Calendar

October

	Sunday	Monday	Tuesday	Wednesday	Thursday	Friday	Saturday

Planning Calendar

November

November	Sunday	Monday	Tuesday	Wednesday	Thursday	Friday	Saturday

ShortCuts for Fall ©1992 Monday Morning Books, Inc.

Weekly Calendar Frieze

September

MONTH

MONDAY

TUESDAY

WEDNESDAY

THURSDAY

FRIDAY

Weekly Calendar Frieze

October

MONTH

MONDAY

TUESDAY

WEDNESDAY

THURSDAY

FRIDAY

Weekly Calendar Frieze

November

MONTH

MONDAY

TUESDAY

WEDNESDAY

THURSDAY

FRIDAY

Birthday Chart
September

SEPTEMBER BIRTHDAYS

Birthday Chart
September

HAPPY BIRTHDAY!

Birthday Chart
October

OCTOBER BIRTHDAYS

Birthday Chart
October

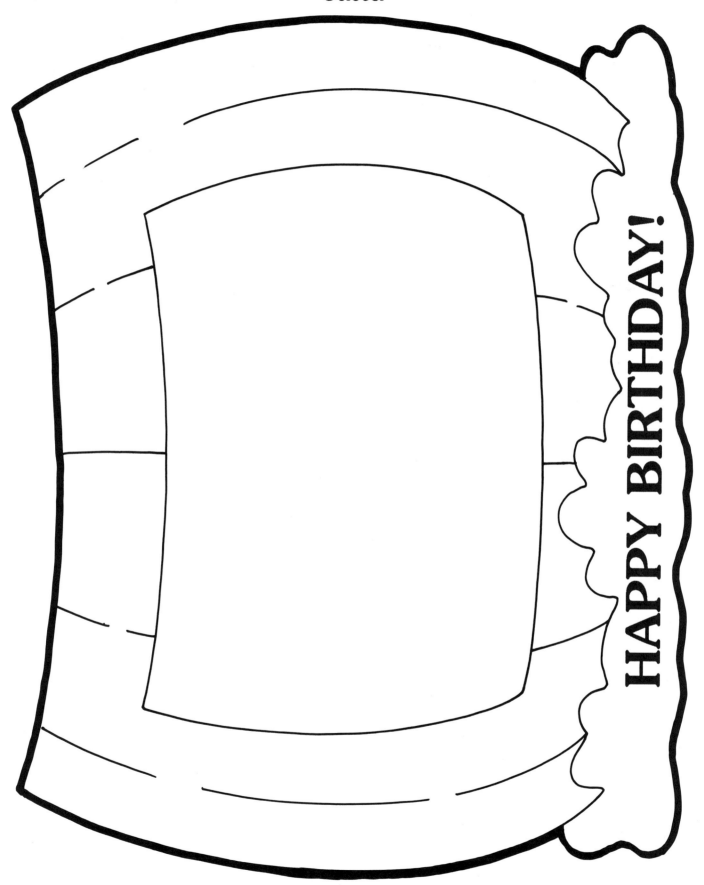

HAPPY BIRTHDAY!

Birthday Chart
November

Birthday Chart
November

HAPPY BIRTHDAY!

Scrapbook Page

SEPTEMBER

Scrapbook Page

OCTOBER

ShortCuts for Fall ©1992 Monday Morning Books, Inc.

Scrapbook Page

NOVEMBER

 **Seating Chart**
September

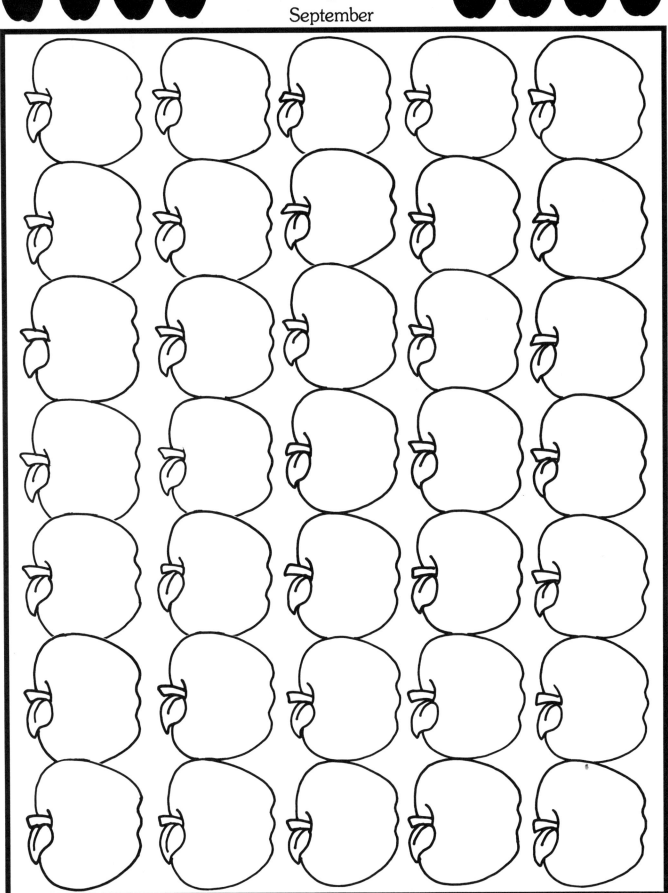

Seating Chart
October

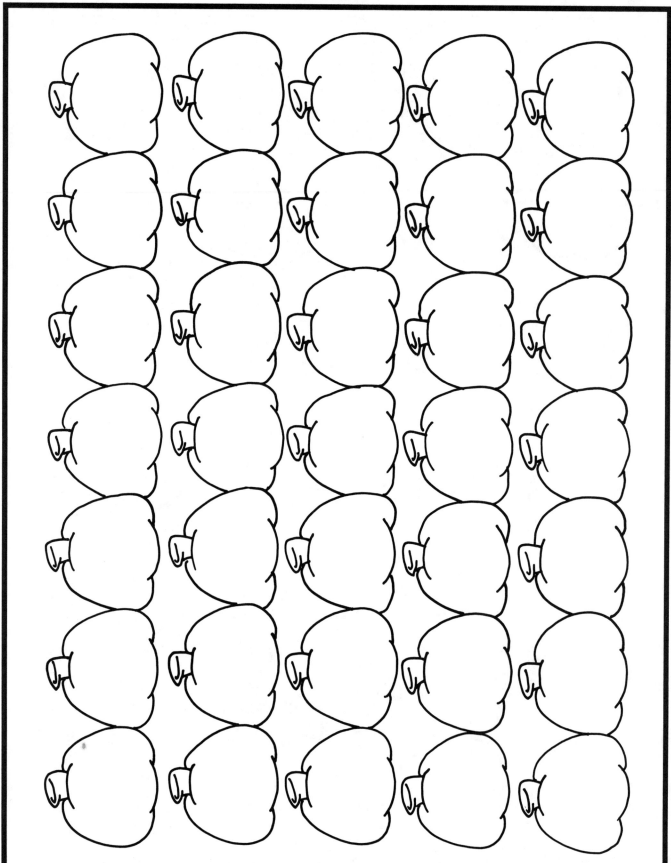

44

 # Seating Chart
November

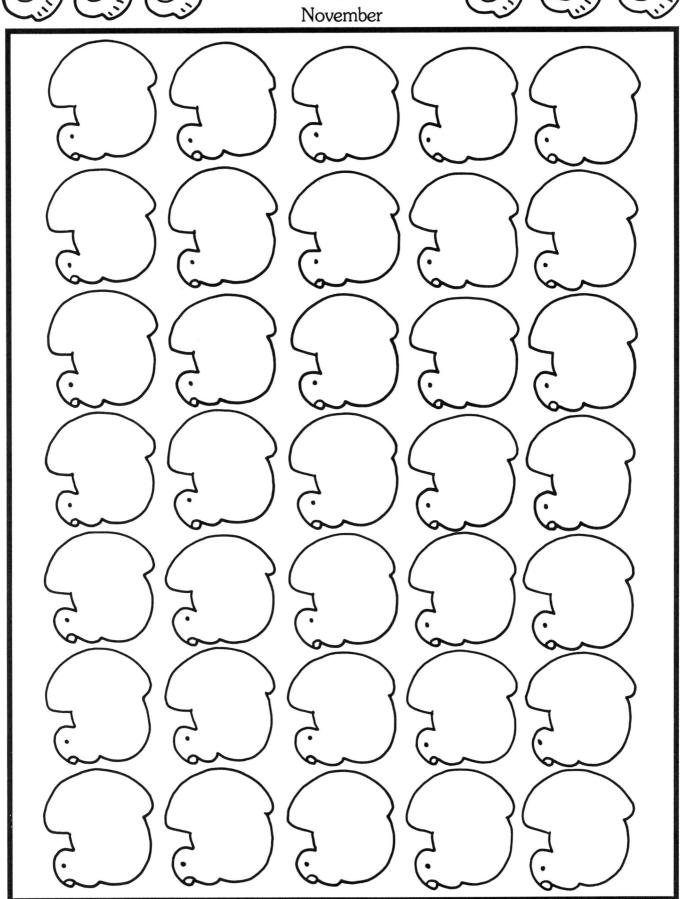

Attendance Chart
September

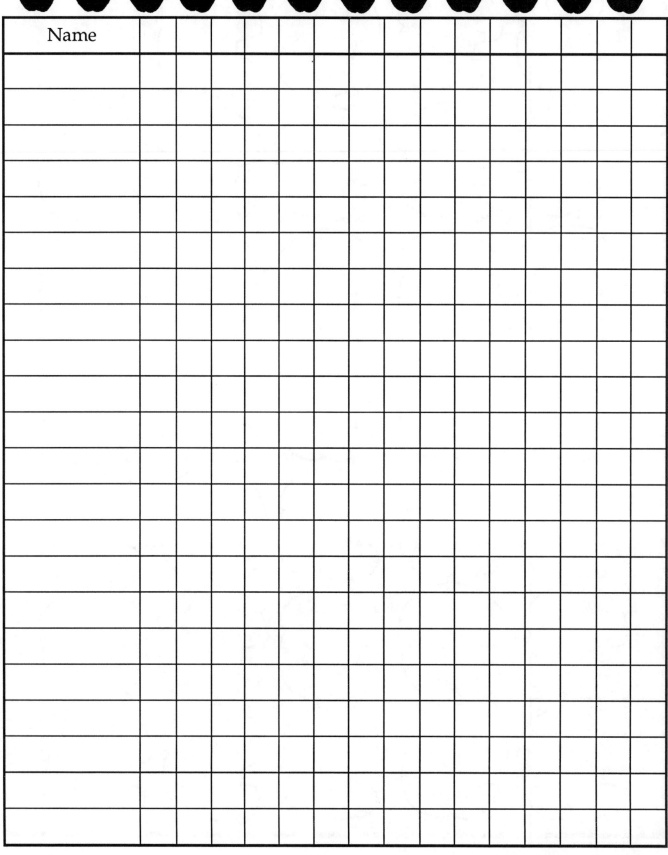

Name												

Attendance Chart
October

Name										

Attendance Chart
November

Name															

Open Chart

Substitute Teacher Agenda

Lesson Plan   Mr./Ms. _____ Class

_____
_____
_____
_____
_____
_____
_____
_____
_____
_____

Special Information

_____
_____
_____
_____

Students with Special Classes

_____
_____
_____
_____
_____
_____
_____
_____
_____
_____
_____

Classroom Helpers

_____
_____
_____
_____
_____
_____
_____
_____

Name _____

Name _____

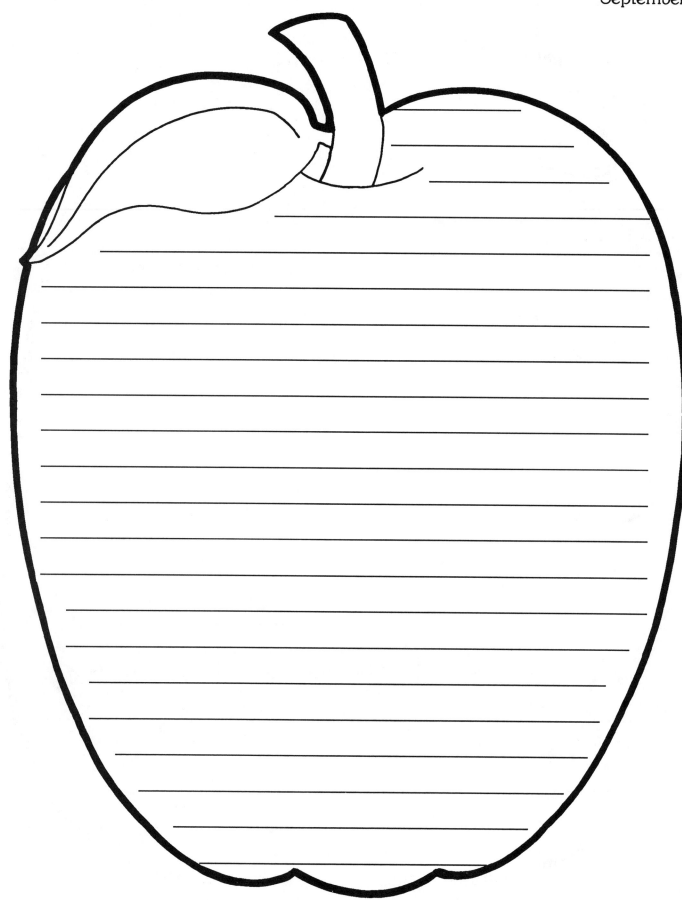

Worksheet Display Banner September

We're Proud
of
Good Work!

To display student work,
cut out the banner and
slit along dotted lines.
Then slip worksheet
under paws and secure.

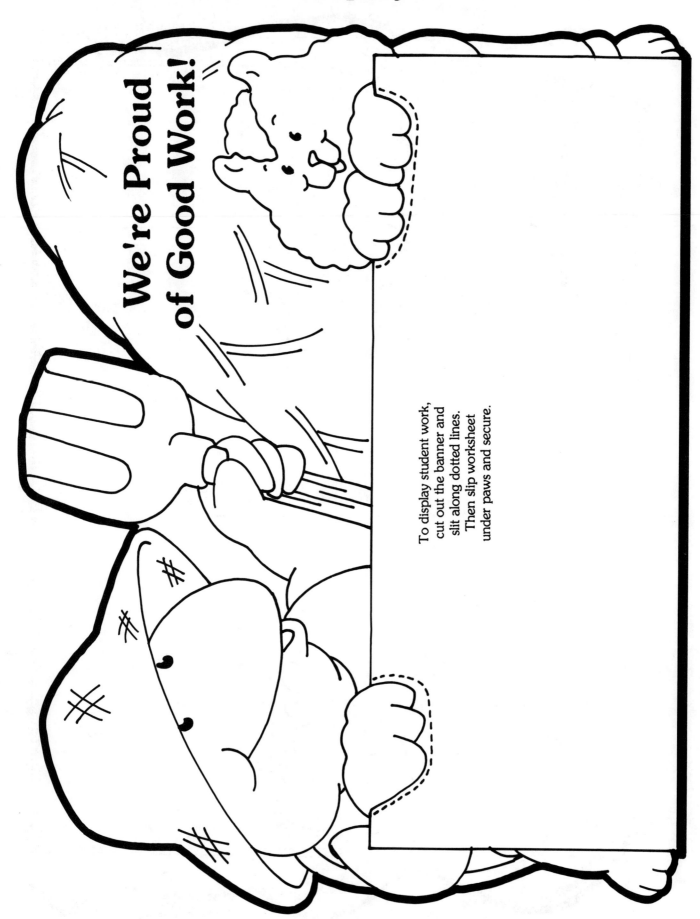

We're Proud of Good Work!

To display student work, cut out the banner and slit along dotted lines. Then slip worksheet under paws and secure.

Worksheet Display Banner November

We're Proud
of
Good Work!

To display student work,
cut out the banner and
slit along dotted lines.
Then slip worksheet
under paws and secure.

Newsletter Cover

Teacher's Name _____ Class

City _____ , State _____

Published _____ times per _____

Newsletter Section Titles

Editorial Staff

In This Issue
NEWS TODAY

A Message From...

EXTRA CREDIT OPPORTUNITIES

The Chatterbox

Welcome Special Guests

Spotlight

Things to Remember

The Letter Box

World News Report

Birthdays

The Kitchen Log

Local News

Homework Hotline

ShortCuts for Fall ©1992 Monday Morning Books, Inc.

File Folder Cover

September

IN THIS FOLDER

☐ Homework
☐ Math
☐ Social Studies
☐ Spelling Words
☐ Other _____

☐ Class Work
☐ Science
☐ Language Arts
☐ Book Report

File Folder Cover

October

IN THIS
FOLDER

- ☐ Homework
- ☐ Math
- ☐ Social Studies
- ☐ Spelling Words
- ☐ Class Work
- ☐ Science
- ☐ Language Arts
- ☐ Book Report
- ☐ Other _____

IN THIS FOLDER

- ☐ Homework
- ☐ Math
- ☐ Social Studies
- ☐ Spelling Words
- ☐ Class Work
- ☐ Science
- ☐ Language Arts
- ☐ Book Report
- ☐ Other _____

Name Tags/Flashcards

September

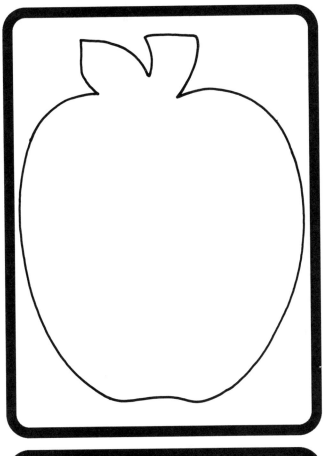

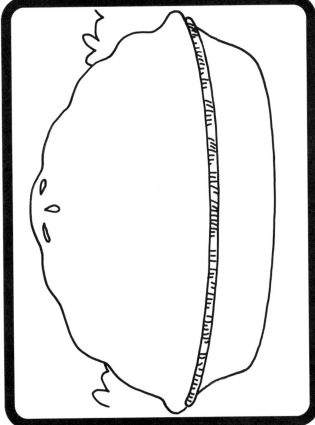

Name Tags/Flashcards

October

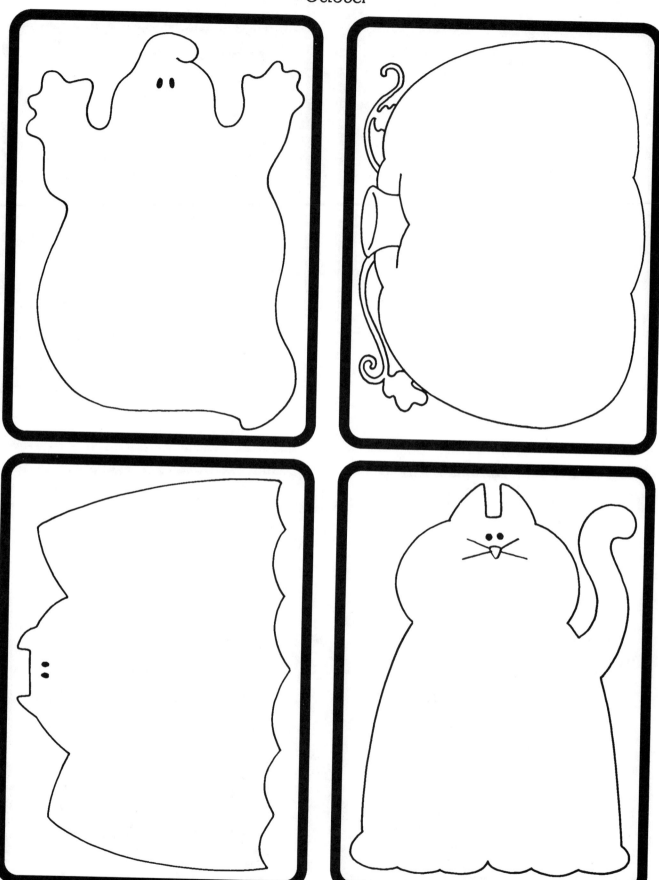

Name Tags/Flashcards
November

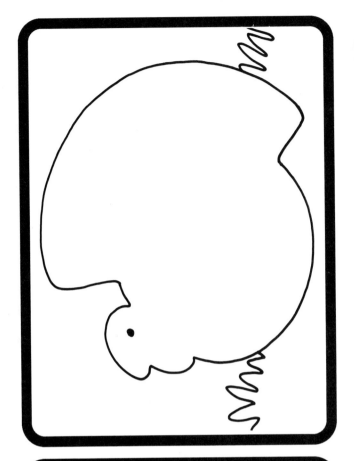

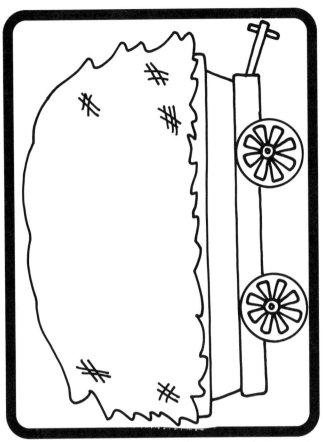

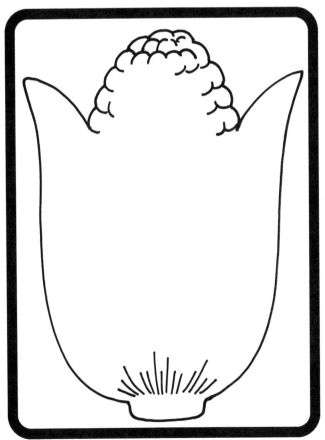

Doorknob Hangers & Hall Passes

Teacher _____

Date _____

HALL PASS

Teacher _____

Date _____

HALL PASS

Bookmarks

Good Books to Read!

Good
Books
to Read!

Good
Books
to Read!

Good
Books
to Read!

ShortCuts for Fall ©1992 Monday Morning Books, Inc.

Bookmarks
My Favorite Books!

My
Favorite
Books!

My
Favorite
Books!

My
Favorite
Books!

ShortCuts for Fall ©1992 Monday Morning Books, Inc.

Bookmarks

I Love Books!

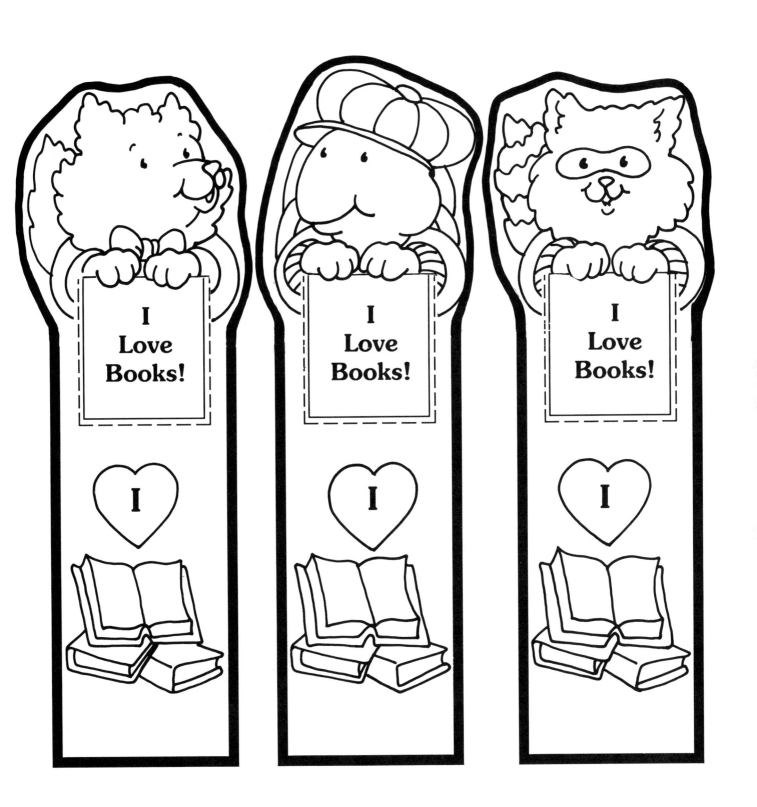

ShortCuts for Fall ©1992 Monday Morning Books, Inc.

Pencil Awards
Great Work!

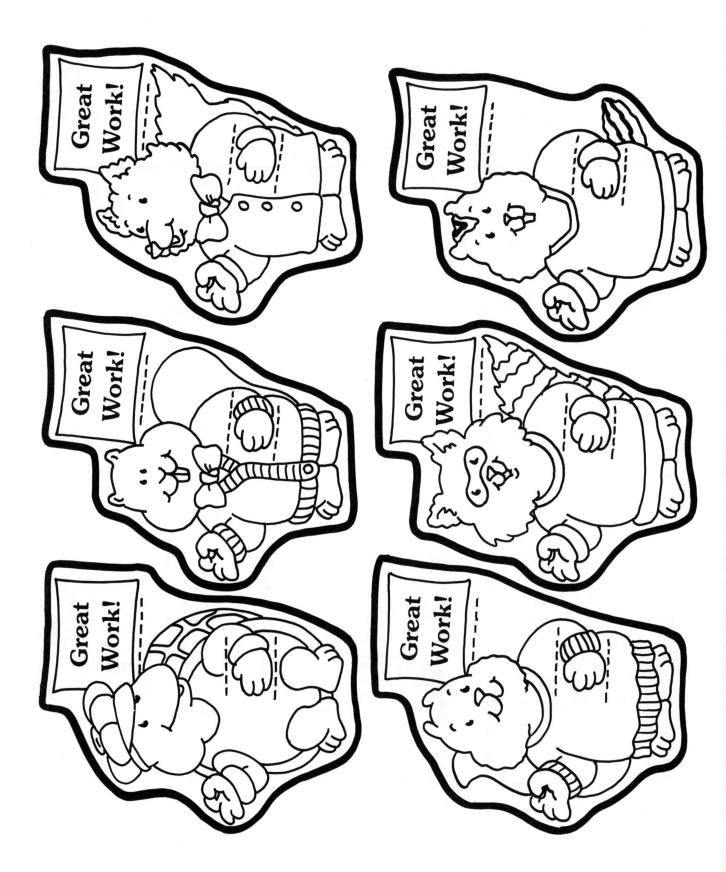

Button Awards

I Do Good Work!

I Do
Good
Work!

Name

I Do
Good
Work!

Name

I Do
Good
Work!

Name

I Do
Good
Work!

Name

Button Awards

I Do Good Work!

I Do
Good
Work!

Name

I Do
Good
Work!

Name

I Do
Good
Work!

Name

I Do
Good
Work!

Name

74

Headband/Wristband Awards

Fall

Use Strip **A** for wristband awards.
Use strips **B**, **C**, and **D** for headband awards.

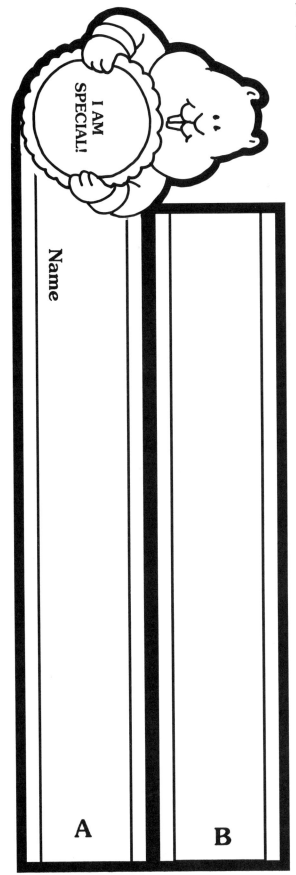

I AM
SPECIAL!

Name

A

B

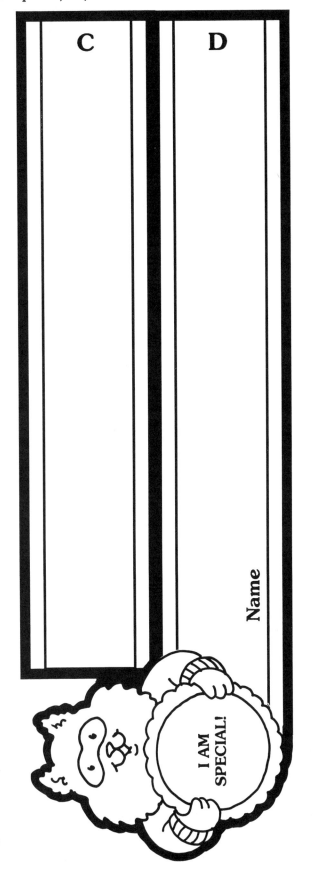

C

D

I AM
SPECIAL!

Name

Club Card & Coupon Awards

Fall

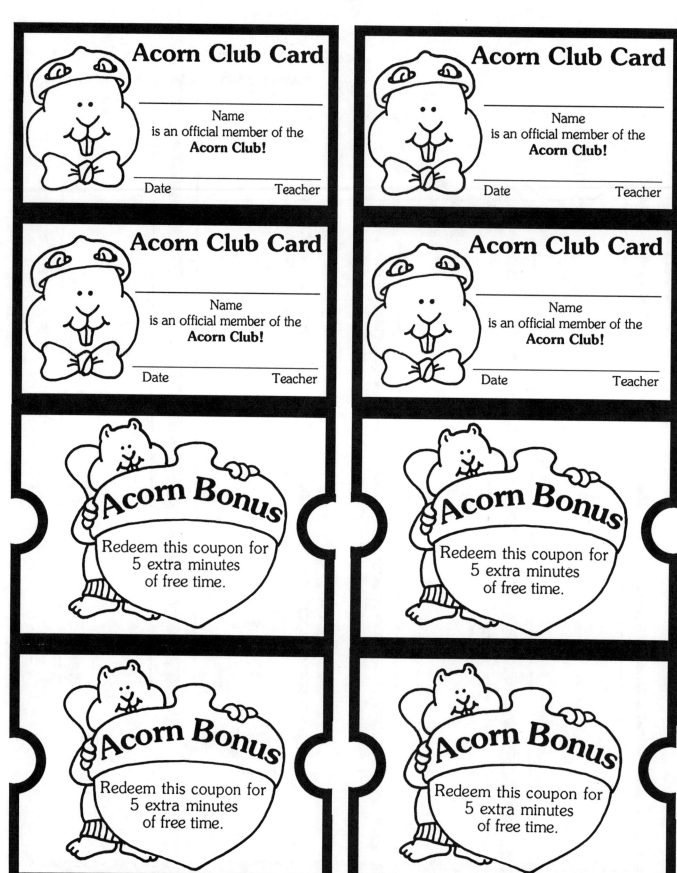

Acorn Club Card

_____
Name
is an official member of the
Acorn Club!
_____
Date   Teacher

Acorn Club Card

_____
Name
is an official member of the
Acorn Club!
_____
Date   Teacher

Acorn Club Card

_____
Name
is an official member of the
Acorn Club!
_____
Date   Teacher

Acorn Club Card

_____
Name
is an official member of the
Acorn Club!
_____
Date   Teacher

Acorn Bonus
Redeem this coupon for
5 extra minutes
of free time.

Acorn Bonus
Redeem this coupon for
5 extra minutes
of free time.

Acorn Bonus
Redeem this coupon for
5 extra minutes
of free time.

Acorn Bonus
Redeem this coupon for
5 extra minutes
of free time.

ShortCuts for Fall ©1992 Monday Morning Books, Inc.

Booklet Award
FOR A JOB WELL DONE!

Big Red Apple Diploma

The **BIG RED APPLE**

DIPLOMA

is
presented
to

Name

Date

Teacher

Big Acorn Diploma

This **BIG ACORN** DIPLOMA

is presented to

Name

Teacher

Date

Horn of Plenty Diploma

The Horn of Plenty Diploma

This diploma is awarded to

Name

Date

Teacher

ShortCuts for Fall ©1992 Monday Morning Books, Inc.